Destination
Prince Edward Island
Its Culture and Landscapes

Photography: Anne MacKay
Text: Shauna McCabe

NIMBUS
PUBLISHING

Nimbus Publishing Limited
PO Box 9301, Station A
Halifax, NS   B3K 5N5
(902) 455-4286

Design: Graphic Detail Inc., Charlottetown, PEI

Front Cover: Field of bright lupins, at Clinton. The lupin has become an unofficial symbol of Prince Edward Island.
Back Cover: The Island landscape, with its backroads, rolling fields, and beaches, is a recreational paradise and rich reservoir of stories. Off the main route, cyclists tour near lower Bedeque.
Title Page: Sunrise at Nine Mile Creek.

Printed and bound in Canada

Canadian Cataloguing in Publication Data
McCabe, Shauna, 1967-
ISBN 1-55109-324-3
1. Prince Edward Island – Description and travel.
2. Prince Edward Island – History.   I. MacKay, Anne.   II. Title.
FC2617.4 M32 2000   971.7   C99-950265-4   F1047.M32 2000

Nimbus Publishing acknowledges financial support for its publishing activities from the Government of Canada through the Book Publishing Industry Development Program (BPIDP), and the Canada Council.

Lessons about how landscape is inseparable from memory and its "old maps" are stumbled upon all over this Island. This is dedicated to a place called Millcove.

–Shauna McCabe

ACKNOWLEDGEMENTS

The author would like to acknowledge the following for granting permission to reprint selections from published works: An excerpt of Milton Acorn's poem, "The Figure in the Landscape made the Landscape" has been reprinted with kind permission from Mary Hooper, literary executor for Milton Acorn. Kind permission to incorporate passages of "North Shore Poem," by Frank Ledwell, "The Boats of Murray Harbour," words and music by David Weale, "The Ice Boat Song," words and music by Wendell Boyle, and "Your Island Will Disappear," words and music by Allan Rankin, has been granted by the authors. L. M. Montgomery's poem, "Twilight in Abegweit" is cited with permission from David Macdonald and Ruth Macdonald. L. M. Montgomery is a trademark of the Heirs of L. M. Montgomery Inc. "Song of the Irish Moss," words and music by Tom Connors, © copyright 1971 Crown Vetch Music, is used with permission.

Thanks from Anne MacKay to: Orwell Corner Historic Village, Point Prim lighthouse, The Inn at Bay Fortune, Prince Edward Island Department of Tourism, Patricia Murray and St. Mary's Church, The Indian River Festival, The Farmers' Bank in South Rustico, Parks Canada, Joan Cummin, The Festival of the Fathers, Doug Prothero, Confederation Centre of the Arts, La Promenade Acadienne, The Acadian Festival, Abrams Village, Eptek National Exhibition Centre, Alberton Museum, St. Simon and St. Jude Catholic Churches, The Prince County Exhibition, Basin Head Fisheries Museum, Elmira Railway Museum.

Special thanks to: Wayne Barrett who contributed four photographs to this project, page x, 2, 44 and 54.

Table of Contents

Map of Prince Edward Island IV

Introduction V

Hills and Harbours 1

Bays and Dunes 9

Anne's Land 17

Charlotte's Shore 25

Charlottetown 33

Ship to Shore 41

Sunsets and Seascapes 49

Wild thyme in fall abundance.

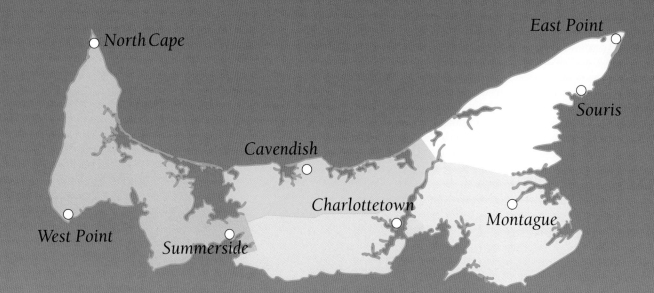

East Point

North Cape

Souris

Cavendish

Charlottetown

Montague

West Point

Summerside

N

Anne's Land

Bays & Dunes

Charlotte's Shore

Hills & Harbours

Sunsets & Seascapes

Ship to Shore

Introduction

There are some basic laws of geography. One is that islands are different. "Islands," says writer David Quammen, are "havens and breeding grounds for the unique and anomalous." Whether ecologically, culturally, historically, or socially, the deep water that separates such "outland" places from the inland lends them an essential character that sets them apart, in more ways than just their geographical isolation.

Because of their uniqueness, islands have inevitably captured the imagination. An island's inherent separation makes it an insular retreat, a hideout. Prince Edward Island, the small, crescent-shaped island in the Gulf of the St. Lawrence, is one such place. Long prized as a destination for settlers and an escape for travellers, it has been described as both a garden and playground.

And because of its relatively small size, this island evokes intimacy. It soon becomes familiar; it is knowable. One can navigate Prince Edward Island's well-worn clay roads, come to recognize the shape of its coves and rocky outcrops, learn the location of abundant berry patches and secluded beaches, its treasured views and sacred landmarks. "Nowhere," as Prince Edward Island poet Milton Acorn has written, "is there a spot not measured by hands;/no direction I couldn't walk/to the wave-lined edge of home."

Nowhere, either, is there a spot not measured by imagination, no site that is not steeped in meaning, in history. Prince Edward Island's landscape is remarkable for the sheer wealth of stories, song, prose, poetry, and art it has inspired. Every element of its geography has been described and transcribed: from Mi'kmaq stories of the

These spring fields at Clyde River are among the many lasting marks of PEI's early settlers.

Island's creation, to Jacques Cartier's sixteenth-century observations of shallow water, sandbanks, and the wooded landscape; from Lucy Maud Montgomery's memorable evocations of the north shore, to Robert Harris's paintings of Island settings and figures, to poetry and music that capture a sense of place such as Milton Acorn's "Minago," and singer Stompin' Tom Connors's "Skinner's Pond."

> *And the landscape rolling like a quilt*
> *By one of those strange fitnesses*
> *Of geography and history*
> *Is red and green, red and green, two rebellious colours;*
> *Clearings and woodlots, clearings and woodlots....*
>
> "The Figure in the Landscape Made the Landscape"
> Milton Acorn

In these words and images are clues to the layered meanings of many Island landscapes and landmarks. In a way, they provide pictures of this place and its past. And they offer imaginative maps of the markings etched by centuries of activity and people who have left their impression on its surface. Every landmark has a story and a history. If you look closely, then, you can find the Island's biography, an account of the interaction of history and geography that made the cultural landscape around us today.

PEI's physical geography has both offered possibilities and imposed limits to the way it has evolved. The proximity of the sea has always influenced Island ways of life. As well, the irregular shoreline heavily indented by estuarial bays and coves has, over the centuries, offered natural harbours for settlement. Across the island, rivers and streams find their way to the sea, mixing with salt water toward their mouths.

Inland, lies a mix of Acadian forest and gentle rolling topography of easily cultivated red clay, which rests over a layer of sandstone. At the edges of the Island, visible evidence of these "redbeds" are found in the distinctive fragile rocky cliffs that run along many Island beaches. The constantly shifting sand that has created the province's

These steep sandstone cliffs at East Point— where the tides of the Atlantic Ocean, Northumberland Strait, and the Gulf of St. Lawrence collide—are carved continuouslyby the sea.

famous white sand beaches and dunes, has also shaped life here. Carried by the wind and water and deposited, sand has sometimes hindered access to harbours. This process of slow physical evolution has been mirrored by the changes in the Island's social, cultural, and demographic realms. Waves of settlers—among them Mi'kmaq, Acadians, Irish, Scottish, British, and later, Black, American, Lebanese, and Dutch—have given the Island's social landscape its contours and textures, shaping it like the sea.

The discovery of artifacts at several sites has established a human presence dating back at least 10,000 years, when the land that later became Prince Edward Island was still joined to the mainland. Here, nomadic Paleo-Indians are believed to have hunted caribou, seal, and walrus, fish and birds. Evidence has also been found supporting a later Island settlement existing between 9,000 and 3,500 years ago, when it was inhabited by Maritime Archaic Indians who took advantage of the rich resources of the sea.

Pottery and piles of shell found on the north shore of the Island indicate subsequent settlers were the Mi'kmaq inhabitants, who knew the Island by the name *Minagoo*. Stories and legends still exist in the Mi'kmaq oral tradition as to how the Island and its landscape took form. In a creation legend as relayed by John Joe Sark, cultural leader and Keptin of the Mi'kmaq Grand Council of the District of Epekwitk, "The great spirit fashioned an enchanting island and called it *Minagoo*. He dressed her dark red skin with green grass and lush forests of many kinds of trees and sprinkled her with many brightly coloured

flowers." The Island was known as well as Abegweit, which, appropriately, means "cradled on the waves."

The Mi'kmaq hunted, fished, and harvested the seasonal resources of the Island, including oysters, clams, various fish and mammals, birds, berries, and nuts. Wood and birchbark from the dense forest that would have covered much of the island was used in the building of canoes, lodges, and containers. The Mi'kmaq community of Prince Edward Island shared fishing and hunting resources in the region with the residents of other native districts. Although this early presence of the native population on the Island was a subtle one, the Mi'kmaq community has remained an important component of the Prince Edward Island landscape.

History attributes the first European encounter with the province to Jacques Cartier in 1534, who recorded the oldest existing written description of the Island. He noted the aboriginal population as well as the natural landscape: "The trees which were wonderfully beautiful and very fragrant....It is the best tempered region one can possibly see and the heat is considerable. There are many turtle-doves, wood-pigeons, and other birds." This "new world" would become very important to Europe. The Gulf of St. Lawrence, the Bay of Fundy, and the Grand Banks of Newfoundland became fishing grounds for fishers from England, France, Spain, Portugal, and Holland.

Though French and Basque fishermen were frequent visitors, settlement of the Island did not really begin until the eighteenth century, when the French began to establish themselves along the Island's coastlines. By 1632, a group of 300 French settlers had arrived in Nova Scotia,

The Kensington Railway Station, one of two "boulder" railway stations on the Island, opened in 1905 and is now the location of the community library. Though Island rails are now trails, many of the old stations have found imaginative new uses.

ancestors of the majority of Acadians in the Maritime region. By 1700, there were more than 1,000 Acadians residing in the region. They often settled in marshland areas, draining and dyking swamps for agricultural land, harvesting marsh hay. The island's first permanent Acadian communities were established along its rivers and the seashore. They called it Île St. Jean, and a small administrative centre was built just inside what is now Charlottetown Harbour, known then as Port La Joie. A major fishing centre was located at the mouth of St. Peter's Bay and other settlements were built at Tracadie, Savage Harbour, and near the Bedeque-Malpeque isthmus. Due to the lack of meadowlands, here too they often drained tidal marsh flats, creating dyked farmlands.

Though insular, the Island has never been isolated; even in the eighteenth century it was affected by events beyond its shores. Both Britain and France wanted to control Acadia because of its strategic location within the Atlantic fisheries and the fur trade of the St. Lawrence River Valley. Acadia became a battleground and this broader English-French struggle had an impact on the Island. The Acadians' increasingly precarious position in Nova Scotia caused many to seek another place to settle. Many crossed the strait to the Island. Over the next five years, the population on the Island grew to over 2,000, and new settlements appeared at Pownal, Orwell, Pinette, Crapaud, Tryon, and Covehead. By 1758, there were more than 4,000 residents, as more Acadians from the Fundy region took refuge on the Island when the expulsion and deportation of Acadians began, following the surrender of Louisbourg to the British.

The Acadian culture managed to survive in the nucleus of those French who escaped expulsion and others who returned, and the Acadians played an important force in shaping the province. The Acadians established fortifications at Port La Joie, along with several hundred houses, saw and grist mills, hundreds of acres of dyked farmland and cleared woodland. They also began the early fisheries. Despite continuing assimilation pressures, Acadians remain a strong presence on Prince Edward Island. Today, many Islanders are of Acadian ancestry and efforts to recover and maintain its linguistic and cultural identity have resulted in a vibrant Acadian cultural and institutional life.

With the end of the French regime, the Island became known as the Island of St. John's, and subsequently, in 1799, Prince Edward Island. New groups of settlers from England, Scotland, and Ireland began to arrive. By 1805, the population had grown from several hundred Mi'kmaq and Acadians to 7,000, and by 1881, there were 109,000 residents, most of English, Scottish, and Irish descent. The change in settlement was also reflected in the look of the land. As the population had grown, the clearing of forest intensified. The land, including that which had been settled by the Acadians, was surveyed and divided into 67 lots or townships. The Island was divided into three counties—Prince, Queens, and Kings—each with its own capital. Roads and fields are still laid out along this grid, giving the Island its distinctive physical layout.

The townships of land were distributed in a land lottery—the Great Lottery of July 1767. In many cases,

Rolling farm fields at Fairview. Since the days of early settlement, farming has been important in shaping the Island landscape.

absentee landlords hoarded the land, creating resentment over the cost of rent. The resulting tensions established between owners and tenants continued until after Confederation when the provincial government bought back the land from the landlords. The "land question"—issues surrounding the public and private use of land—remains an emotional matter today.

Today more than three-quarters of the residents are descendants of early settlers from the British Isles: Highland Scots, English, and southern and Ulster Ireland. Land was cleared of forest, and numerous farms and small rural communities were established. The early settlement of the island was heavily rural. Settlement throughout the countryside was markedly linear along the roads, which, more often than not, followed the original survey orientation.

Charlottetown was long the only village-town centre of any importance and as it grew to urban status, another town, Summerside, developed on the south shore. Communities tended to be remote; ethnic groups mainly settled in their own small, isolated coastal communities, following religious lines. The countless sheltered harbours along the coastline were perfect for settlements, though in some areas of the north shore, sand dunes often barred entrances to bays and rivers. The natural harbours also facilitated a thriving ship-building industry; from 1780 to 1890 about 4,500 sailing vessels were built. Shipyards existed on virtually every bay and river. But the "golden age" of sail came to a close when wood resources dwindled and steam ships

built with steel replaced sailing vessels. Mills also flourished on the Island's rivers and streams. In 1871, there were more than 500 mills—shingle, sawlogs, grist, woolen, and dressing mills—set up on ponds. In the late 1800s, the Island supported 100,000 people, living primarily on 15,000 farms. The general patterns on the land—the lay of the roads, patchwork of fields, estuarial bays, which became fishing ports, and county divisions—still exist today.

During the late nineteenth century, Lebanese and American Blacks also became part of the cultural landscape. These groups along with twentieth-century immigrants from Holland, Guatemala, East India, China, Germany, El Salvador, and other locations have added to the diversity of the province's languages and customs.

Further dramatic changes were precipitated by a meeting to discuss the union of the Maritime provinces. The Island's status grew with the Charlottetown meeting of the Fathers of Confederation, preparing the way for the Quebec Conference in 1864, and the founding of the Dominion of Canada that followed. Prince Edward Island has since been known as the "Cradle of Confederation." The Island, however, did not join Confederation until 1873, and then only with hesitation. The federal government promised the completion of the trans-Island railway that the Island government had begun in 1871, fulfilling the federal guarantee of continuous communication with the mainland. The railway, in service by 1875, curved through the middle of the Island's countryside. Ottawa began ferry service to the Island in

1875. The ferries initially ran between Georgetown, PEI and Pictou County in Nova Scotia, and Summerside, PEI and Point du Chêne, New Brunswick. These new transportation routes encouraged the further settlement and development of networks of roads.

Although today agriculture continues to serve as the economic base and the key shaper of the landscape, farms number less than 1,000. PEI's population of 137,000 is more urban-oriented. Shipbuilding waned and gave way to other industries, but private woodlots still yield hardwood and softwood for lumber, plywood, and fuel. Fishing continues to be important, depending primarily on lobster catch, but mussels, oysters, clams, and scallops are other sea resources. A secondary industry is the harvesting of Irish moss, a seaweed, to extract carrageenan. The Island tourism economy has also grown dramatically over the last century.

Such development has put pressure on the relatively unspoiled, pristine landscapes that have always been a treasured part of the Island. The Island struggles to balance this with preserving an uncommodified natural beauty and an emphasis on intimacy and living close to the land, which are also important values here. Despite all the changes over the past centuries, there has been continuity in the issues that draw passion–land use, sustainable development, and the health of resources are basic precepts that have linked the Island, through its history and migrations.

These values and issues have drawn new groups of settlers, people with environmental concerns, artists, and craftspeople, who are attracted to the intimacy and small-scale character of the place. This has been paralleled during the last several decades in a resurgence in heritage practices, traditional music, and crafts, such as pottery, weaving, quilting, and metalwork.

While nothing in modern life stands still, on Prince Edward Island somehow it may seem to. One can touch the past everywhere—in the fields, lighthouses, and little white churches that dot the landscape, in lobster fishing boats coming into a harbour, in the harvesting of Irish moss and digging of clams on sandbars, in the pattern of clay roads and the farmhouses that lie along them, in harness races, in house parties, farmers' markets, and strawberry socials.

And yet everywhere tradition meets change. Trains have been displaced by cars and trucks; one of the regular ferry service routes between the Island and New Brunswick was replaced by the Confederation Bridge, stretching across the Northumberland Strait, completed in 1997. Old houses are now bed and breakfast accommodations and inns, old rails have become trails, traditional crafts like quilting and weaving are now featured in gift

Horses are still used in the harvesting of Irish moss, which is raked from the surf along the Island's shores.

shops, and across the province, tradition is celebrated and reconstructed in festivals each year.

The future of the Island is clearly tied tightly to its past. Its rich cultural background, natural beauty, and diverse geography continue to attract new visitors, who in turn become familiar with the Island's landmarks, myths, and histories. Despite its small size and peaceful, unassuming presence, Prince Edward Island has a powerful hold on the individual, visitor, and resident alike. Images of the Island's pleasing landscape—its gently rolling hills, farmed fields of red soil, seaside fishing communities, pioneer graveyards, sand-duned and "wave-lined edges"—imprint themselves on the memory. These compelling images of a picturesque landscape are often, unsurprisingly, picture-perfect and mark locations that demand to be re-visited. As poet Douglas Malcolm asks, "Red roads, green fields /become in paint /red roads, and green fields/What is it about this place that invites cliché?"

Hills and Harbours

The Island way of life has been shaped by the ever-present shore, defining the Island physically and psychologically. Living on the threshold of land and sea has been central to the experience of the region referred to as Hills and Harbours, traditionally called Southern King's County. For 300 years, ships have brought people to and from the southeastern part of the Island. Early in its settlement, these would have been Acadian, and then Irish or Scottish settlers. Before the building of the first Hillsborough Bridge, a paddle-wheel ferry was the only direct route from Charlottetown across the Hillsborough River. Fishing boats, sailing ships, boats transporting wood to mills have all navigated the shoreline. Today, the Northumberland ferry still runs to Wood Islands on the eastern end of PEI.

On the eastern south shore, the Northumberland Strait runs along a ragged coastline, indented with bays. Lighthouses such as those at Wood Islands and Beach Point stand on headlands guiding fishing and other vessels, central to life built around edge of the sea and land. The oldest lighthouse on the Island is located at Point Prim, a long cape that juts out into the Northumberland Strait that was once called "Pointe à Prime" by French settlers. Built in 1845–1846, Point Prim lighthouse on its quiet beach was the only circular brick lighthouse in Canada, though it has since been covered with wood. Here, stories still circulate of a persistent ghost, a hunched figure making his way along the shoreline with an intricately carved shovel. The figure is said to be an Acadian who was forced to leave with the expulsion and drowned on the *Violet*, one of two ships carrying exiled Acadians to France, which went down in the Atlantic, when the ship returned for buried treasure. The bays along the Northumberland Strait have been the location of many phantom ship sightings.

The French were the first settlers of the area around Pownal, Orwell, and Pinette Bays, on both sides of Point Prim. The shores and waterways were often considered valuable places for French settlement. The area of Brudenell is the site of the "Three Rivers" settlement. The area where the Brudenell, Montague, and Cardigan Rivers flow into Cardigan Bay were settled by a group of 300 French led by Jean Pierre de la Roma in 1732. They cleared the woods, levelled the land, built houses, harvested crops, and fished. The area of the confluence of the rivers provided one of the finest harbours on the Island. After the fall of Louisbourg in 1745, the community was destroyed by the British.

On this indented coastline, wherever there was a bay there was frequently a harbour and settlement. Montague, the largest town and government centre of King's County, developed as the head of navigation and centre for shipping. The town grew around the bridge from which ships were loaded with Island potatoes and produce. As the interior was settled, Montague helped to bring goods to market by sail. As in nearby Georgetown, wharves and fishery buildings reflect a life built around the sea. In the mid-1800s, the Georgetown shipyards saw the launching of scores of wooden sailing vessels. Once the community's mainstay, Georgetown's is now the Island's only functioning shipyard.

Oh! the comin' and the goin'
of those little lobster boats,
all rigged and set
with crates and bait
and buoy lines and floats.
They swing their bows into the wind
when the groaner clears his throat,
those briny little boats
from Murray Harbour.

"The Boats of Murray Harbour"
David Weale

A draught horse grazes at Guernsey Cove.

Facing page: Evidence of a life along shore: lobster traps now rest in an Island garden.

Inland, the southeastern shore is heavily wooded. There is more forested acreage in King's County than the other two counties, and the hills are marked by rivers and streams. Along these water systems, mill ponds were at one time the key cultural and economic centres of communities. In the 1800s, many mills were established on the middle courses of streams and the Cardigan, Brudenell and Montague Rivers. Though the majority of mills have disappeared, some are still in operation. From Murray River and another settlement to the south at Murray Harbour, lumber and ships were moving outward in a steady stream. Today, the countryside is hilly and still covered with lush woods, mostly naturally regenerated coniferous and deciduous forests. Wood is still an important resource to the area. Macphail Homestead at Orwell has an experimental forestry project, demonstration woodlots exist at Auburn and Valleyfield, and wood provides material to many local craftspeople.

The region was also the centre of Scottish history on the Island. Migration from Scottish Highlands began in the 1770s. In 1803, Thomas Douglas, fifth Earl of Selkirk, coordinated the move of 800 Scots largely from the Isle of Skye to the Belfast area of Prince Edward Island's southeastern shore. A monument to the early Selkirk settlers stands at Lord Selkirk Provincial Park, the site of PEI's annual Highland Games. These settlers began a wave of Scottish immigration to the area. The Polly Cemetery along the road to Point Prim is the burial site for many of these settlers, named for the *Polly*, one of three vessels that brought them to the area.

The Scottish character and cultural heritage of this corner of the Island was thus set. This is clear in the names that dot the landscape: Kinross, Keppoch, Kinlock, Culloden, Murray River, Murray Harbour, Georgetown. Though traditions have changed, they are still strong. A historic village stands at Orwell Corner, settled by pioneers from Scotland. Musical performers are famous for evoking the Scottish musical heritage. Ceilidhs featuring Scottish traditional music and dance are held at Orwell, among other locations.

Fishing boats anchored off the pier in Lower Montague, where the Brudenell and Montague rivers merge. This area was the site of one of PEI's early Acadian settlements.

Facing page: A one-room schoolhouse in the historic village at Orwell Corner is one of the province's many carefully preserved reminders of the past.

A ferry leaves the harbour at Wood Islands on route to Pictou, Nova Scotia. The Northumberland Strait has served as both a connection and barrier to the mainland since mail service began from this location to Pictou, Nova Scotia in 1775.

Facing page: The oldest lighthouse on the Island has kept watch on the Northumberland Strait at Point Prim since 1845. At one time it was the only circular brick lighthouse in Canada; it has since been covered with wood.

All across the province ploughed potato fields, like this one at Guernsey Cove, stretch out to the water.

Bays and Dunes

"Bays and dunes" aptly describes the perimeter of Eastern King's County. Along the north side, the shoreline stretching from Savage Harbour, to St. Peter's Bay, and along the coast to East Point is rugged and treed. Dunes have in some places been replaced by sandstone cliffs. Southward along the Northumberland Strait, through Basin Head to Cardigan, the coast is marked by coastal inlets and bays, capes and points, and white, shifting dunes.

Here too, settlement has occurred mainly along the coast, encouraged by natural harbours. From Cardigan to Souris are a series of bays along the Northumberland Strait. Areas such as Souris were settled in the early eighteenth century by Acadians, receiving its name from several plagues of mice that beset the area's early French settlers. Today, the community is a busy fishing port and terminal for the Magdalen Islands ferries, which dock there. Most of these communities have historically been dependent on fishing, like Annandale and Launching, named for the sandbar used by fishermen as a launching place.

The traditional fishing character of locations has changed over time. To the east lies Basin Head, with beautiful white beaches, and their "singing sands"—sands that seem to sing underfoot. Here, the fishing wharf is no longer active. Because of shifting offshore sands, fishers have moved to the Souris and North Lake Harbours. The old fishery buildings now house the Basin Head Fisheries Museum, an interpretive centre exploring the Island's inshore fishing industry. They also include an old cannery, saltbox factory, and reconstructed bait sheds.

Barren capes
bravely presuming their way
out to open sea
at MacIntyre's Cove
Naufrage and Sutherland's Landing.
Places passed over
even by detailed maps,
but places nonetheless...

"North Shore Poem"
Frank Ledwell

The solitude and character of many of the Island's outlying areas have been attractive to the cultural community. Actors and writers have resided in Bay Fortune for much of the last century. The first summer actors' colony was established here around the beginning of the twentieth century by Charles P. Flockton. The colony was later home to Elmer Harris, the American playwright who wrote *Johnny Belinda*. Harris's residence subsequently belonged to late Canadian actor Colleen Dewhurst and her husband George C. Scott, and it now houses one of PEI's most popular hotels, the Inn at Bay Fortune. Along a trail near Bay Fortune beach is a sundial in which rest the ashes of Flockton.

At the eastern tip of this region, the East Point lighthouse built in 1867 overlooks the spot where three tides meet, that of the Atlantic Ocean, Northumberland Strait, and the Gulf of St. Lawrence. The sea is a powerful, sometimes treacherous force and this area has been the site of many shipwrecks and fables of buried treasure. Continuing along the north coast, toward Cable Head, the shoreline has also been the site of many shipwrecks, a number of which were lost in the storm of 1906. The name of the community of Naufrage comes from the French word for shipwreck. Nearby is Shipwreck Point.

The French settled the north coast and fished in its bays. The area is home to numerous fishing harbours; fishing wharves are central to sites like Red Head Harbour, Morell, Savage Harbour, Naufrage, North Lake Harbour, and St. Peter's Bay. All along the north shore are red clay roads leading from the main road to the sea, along with blueberry, strawberry, and raspberry patches.

Harboured boats at North Lake.

Facing page: The area around the Inn at Bay Fortune has attracted artists and writers for over a century, inspiring much creative work. The building was originally the residence of Elmer Harris, who wrote Johnny Belinda, *a popular play that has been performed as part of the Charlottetown Festival.*

A blueberry festival takes place in St. Peter's in August; Morell features a strawberry festival in July.

St. Peters was the site of one of the first European settlements on the Island, on the inner shore of the expanse of St. Peter's Bay. It is claimed that in 1719, shipwrecked settlers may have made their homes on the bay, a year before the French settlement at Port La Joie. Many French settled here and down to the east towards Naufrage Harbour. When British control began and the land was parcelled and auctioned off, French family names continued to characterize the area. The bay supported mussel-mud digging, the mussel-mud was then spread on the fields from the 1800s into the 1900s. The area was also an important shipbuilding centre from 1820 to 1870, but declined after the railway was established in the 1870s. Today, aquaculture takes place in St. Peter's Bay. Nearby is Greenwich, the site of beautiful dunes that are overtaking the wooded landscape. The spectacular natural area, with its fragile environmental, cultural, and historical resources is the newest addition to the Prince Edward Island National Park.

Farmer and well-known songmaker Lawrence Doyle, born in 1847, lived in Fortune Road, in the area east of St. Peter's. As part of the Island's musical tradition, his songs, such as "The Merchants of the Bay" and "When Johnny Went Plowing for Kearon" reflect his community roots. Music on the Island is also a vehicle for satire and critique. Another of Doyle's songs, "Prince Edward Isle, Adieu," deals with post-Confederation sentiment on Prince Edward Island by comparing the situation to the earlier land question:

There is a band within this land
Who live in pomp and pride;
To swell their stores they rob the poor;
On pleasures' wings they ride,
With dishes fine their tables shine,
They live in princely style,
Those are the knaves who made us slaves,
And sold Prince Edward Isle.

Today, Doyle has a popular place in the fine tradition of Island songwriting. Culturally and historically, the area is also known for its strong fiddling tradition. The Rollo Bay Fiddle Festival is a significant occasion for fiddlers across the Maritimes. At Monticello, along the north shore, ceilidhs are regular events.

At Basin Head, fisheries buildings now house the Basin Head Fisheries Museum operated by the Prince Edward Island Museum and Heritage Foundation. Once a working harbour, most fishers relocated to Souris and North Lake harbours because of shifting offshore sands.

Facing page: The eastern tip of the Island offers startling beauty, peaceful open spaces, and protected bays that encompass safe harbours for settlement, as well as secluded beaches, like Little Harbour featured here.

Kayakers explore the waters of the inlet near Souris. The area was named with the French word for mice, because of the several mice infestations that beset the French settlers who arrived in the area in the eighteenth century.

Here at Johnstons River is one of the many secluded dirt roads running to the north shore, traditionally used by fishers as a route to the sea.

Anne's Land

The region called Anne's Land spans the middle of the province, encompassing a range of striking landscapes and histories. This portion of the north shore of central Prince Edward Island sweeps from Blooming Point and Tracadie to Cabot Park and Kensington. This area is probably known predominantly for the National Park and its wonderful beaches, like Brackley Beach in the east and Cavendish in the west, and rich interpretive programmes. This is also the literary landscape of Lucy Maud Montgomery. Tourism sites abound, from the house commemorating *Anne of Green Gables*, to amusement parks like Rainbow Valley and the Sandspit.

At its eastern end, the area is bordered by the upper reaches of the Hillsborough River, which was a route of travel used by the Mi'kmaq and other early settlers. Along this National Heritage River are the communities of Scotchfort and Frenchfort. At Scotchfort stands a memorial commemorating the Scottish settlers who landed here in 1772 and established much of this side of the upper river. Here are remains of wharves for schooners built during the age of sail. These riverbanks were also the location of French settlements and a fortification in the 1700s.

The Island's north shoreline was the site of early Acadian, Scottish, Irish, and English settlements. Tracadie Bay evolved as a major fishing inlet, the site of Acadian and Scottish settlement. John MacDonald moved seventeen Scottish families to the area of Corran Ban, Winter River, and Tracadie in 1772. Today, there are traces still of these early cultural influences. The cemeteries at Tracadie and Donaldston have the gravesites of some of the earliest Scottish settlers in this area and of families who have resided in the area for generations. Near Stanhope, founded by Sir James Montgomery in 1770, a pioneer cemetery dating to the early 1800s can be seen along the trailhead to the Farmlands and Bubbling Springs Trails in the National Park. As well, long ridges in the earth there still mark the dykes that edged farm fields.

The Gulf Shore Parkway winds from Dalvay to Robinson's Island through the National Park, along woodlands and the shoreline with its back dunes with their marram grass, bays, barachois ponds, and saltmarshes. The park has had an important presence on the Island since its establishment in 1937, encouraging land conservation, as well as the protection of historic sites, of the fragile environments that are always changing due to sand movement and erosion, and of endangered species such as the piping plover. Interpretive programmes have lead to a greater understanding of the cultural, historical, and natural aspects of these coastlines.

To the west is Rustico, an area with a working fishery. This area was settled by Acadians, and the Acadian culture and language is still strong. Anglo Rustio, North Rustico, South Rustico, and Rustico Bay—all are tributes to René Rassicot who settled in the area in 1724. In the area is the Acadian Farmers' Bank, a red sandstone building built in 1863–64, the first client-owned bank in North America. The coastline here was also the setting for rum-running by ships from St. Pierre and Miquelon, as well as the building and launching of tall

A filmy western sky of smoky red,
Blossoming into stars above a sea
Of soft mysterious dim silver spread
Beyond the long gray dunes' serenity:
Where the salt grasses and sea poppies press
Together in a wild loneliness.

"Twilight in Abegweit"
Lucy Maud Montgomery

Some of the Island's traditional clay roads are now protected as heritage roads. Along these tree-canopied stretches are many glimpses of the past, real and fictional.

Facing page: The sun rises over stretches of red sand revealed by low tide at Rustico in the Prince Edward Island National Park. The name Rustico is a tribute to the French settler René Rassicot who settled in the area in 1724, where the Acadian culture has remained strong.

ships, a great source of prosperity on the Island during its age of sail.

In Cavendish, the presence of Lucy Maud Montgomery and images and characters from her classic book, *Anne of Green Gables* are strong. Montgomery was born in New London and raised on the north shore. Visitors can take in sites such as the stone cellar of the farmhouse where Montgomery lived and wrote. The beautiful scenery from Cavendish, west to Park Corner, inspired Montgomery's literary vistas, which in turn has shaped how new visitors see the landscape today. In the western corner of this region is Malpeque, the location of a Mi'kmaq camp before the French settled there in

the 1720s. Cabot Provincial Park on the north shore is a tribute to an unconfirmed contact of explorer John Cabot, and the site for much of the filming of a television series based on Emily, another of Montgomery's characters.

This is the core of the Island's tourism and recreational landscape. There has been an effort to balance development with the need to protect the integrity and beauty that give the land its distinct character. Throughout this region, there is strong environmental awareness among residents living close to the land, who are concerned for the natural landscape, woodlands, and river systems. As well, there are many craftspeople who work with traditional materials and form an important part of the Island's culture and economy.

Interior of historic St. Mary's Church at Indian River. PEI singer, Patricia Murray, performs as part of the Indian River Festival performance series, held each summer.

Facing page: Within the Prince Edward Island National Park, Green Gables has been restored to represent the farm that served as the setting for Lucy Maud Montgomery's novel Anne of Green Gables.

Ground fog rises near an Island sandstone farmhouse at Springfield.

The Acadian Farmers'
Bank at Cymbria, near
Rustico, was built in
1863–1864 from local
red sandstone quarried
and shaped by Island
masons. This, the first
client-owned bank in
North America, was
created by Father
Georges-Antoine
Belcourt and his
parishioners to serve
the Acadian community
in the area, and now
houses a museum.

Destination Prince Edward Island

Cavendish capes at sunset from Orby Head.

Charlotte's Shore

harlotte's Shore is known to Islanders as the South Shore. Farmland and lush rolling hills lie inland, and the shoreline is famed for its red sandstone cliffs and beaches of red sand. This coastline, the closest to the mainland, has traditionally provided central access to the Island. In the 1800s, Cape Traverse was used as the terminal for iceboat crossings to the mainland. Between 1827 and 1918, these iceboats were used to carry mail and people in winter. Here a monument stands to the iceboat crews, a replica of the iceboats that used the "Capes Route." As a result of the Confederation agreement, Ottawa began steamer ferry service to the Island in 1875. In the late 1800s, a proposal was made for a safer tunnel passage under the Northumberland Strait, which never came to fruition. Over the twentieth century, ferry boats have operated, docking at the port community of Borden, carrying passengers, cars, and trucks.

The face of Borden has drastically changed with the completion in May 1997 of the Confederation Bridge. During the 1980s, the subject of a fixed link was frequently raised. In January 1988, a provincial plebiscite was held in the midst of much controversy and debate. With a result of 59 to 41 percent in favour of the bridge, the building of the fixed crossing between Borden and Cape Tormentine, New Brunswick, began in earnest. A monument to the people who captained the ferries, a casualty of this major change, is located at Borden, sculpted from the stones that were once part of the ferry terminal pier.

On a ribbon of red on the shoreline ahead
The church steeple reached up to the sky
What a welcoming sight on this canvas of white,
Like beckoning light from on high.

There's a price you must pay on a cold winter day
If you cross the Northumberland Strait.
And the cost may be grim if you lose life or limb,
For the wind and the tides hold your fate.

"The Ice Boat Song"
Wendell Boyle

At the region's west end is Kensington, a town that developed in the late 1800s as a result of the railway. Kensington was a central point on the train route; Kensington Station opened in 1905, one of only two "boulder" stations on Prince Edward Island. Today it houses a historical display, an information centre, and a craft shop. Kensington serves as an intersection between roads going west to Summerside and beyond, east to Charlottetown, north to Park Corner, northwest to Malpeque and the North Shore.

Along the south shore, fishing villages and rows of cottages dot the coastline. East of Summerside is Bedeque, known as such because the French adapted it from its Mi'kmaq name, *Eptek*. Once a shipbuilding centre, like many communities on the south shore, it remains the site of many potato, dairy, and hog farms. Inland there is a mix of rolling hills, woodlands, and farmland. Old clay roads cross the area, canopied by trees seemingly untouched by time. Today they are protected by law as heritage roads. Communities like Kinkora and Middleton are in the middle of potato growing country. Names such as Kinkora, Emerald, and Shamrock reflect a period of settlement in the early nineteenth century by Irish immigrants.

Evidence of the changing historical geography of the Island can be seen nearby. In the nineteenth century, rivers facilitated the building of mills; streams were dammed to create ponds in order to provide necessary pressure. The Tryon River was once the site of the Island's first woolen mill built by Charles E. Stanfield in 1856. North Tryon was the location of Ives Mill, a sawmill

An apple tree sits
untouched among tilled
fields at Tryon.

Facing page: Blockhouse
Lighthouse at the entrance
to Charlottetown Harbour.
Built in 1876–1877, the
light has guided vessels
into Charlottetown
Harbour and its port
for over a century.

The piers of the Confederation Bridge rise from the Northumberland Strait. The bridge was completed in 1997, marking the passing of an era of ferry service from Borden, Prince Edward Island to Cape Tormentine, New Brunswick.

built in 1860s and demolished in 1977. Such mills were once the economic centres of emerging Prince Edward Island communities. Due to changes in technology and industrialization, they became considered inefficient and obsolete. Some have been transformed to homes or barns, or have become museums or heritage sites. Many others have disappeared.

Similarly, Victoria-by-the-Sea was once an active seaport serving the local agricultural communities. The town declined with the shift from water to land transportation, but has since been revived. Traditional fishery buildings and the wharf have been restored, and the lighthouse is now the location of a museum. The area features a theatre, the Victoria Playhouse, and is home to a small but thriving artistic community.

A vibrant rural arts community is not simply localized in Victoria, but throughout the region many indi-

viduals are involved in different cultural practices. Breadalbane and the area of Dixon Road, for instance, is the location of Malcolm Stanley's pottery studio and is home to many artists and musicians who settled in the area in the 1970s, drawn to the closely knit social atmosphere Prince Edward Island offered.

Towards Charlottetown, in the lower reaches of the Hillsborough River, is Rocky Point. This national historic site was called Port La Joie in the early 1700s when the French established a settlement here. Michel Haché-Gallant, the port captain of Port La Joie and probably the first Acadian to settle on the Island, is buried at the site. When the British took control of the Island, they built Fort Amherst at the same spot. The fort overlooking the harbour was an important strategic site for almost five years. Today, all that is left are earthworks.

Island sandstone house at Clyde River.

The wharves at Victoria-by-the-Sea now house a restaurant and shops. The community is both a working fishing port and a summer resort destination.

A Great Blue Heron on a peaceful creek in Cornwall, in early morning. During summer, these birds seek out the many shallow fresh and salt water areas throughout the Island.

In PEI, red clay is never far beneath the surface: a clay road winds through misty fields near East Wiltshire.

Charlottetown

Surveying the Island to find a location for its capital, Captain Holland saw that Charlottetown was one of the best harbour areas. Tucked inside a narrow entrance, protected by the earlier fortification at Fort Amherst, it offered better opportunities for both transportation and defence than his other choices of Georgetown and Princetown. Earlier, this area along the banks of the three rivers near the harbour had been the site of the first continuous French settlement. The French had hopes of farming the tidal marsh flats along the three estuaries into which the inner harbour of Port la Joie divided.

In 1768, three years after Holland's recommendation, surveyor Charles Morris of Nova Scotia began his town layout. The capital of the colony of St. John's Island was laid out on a grid system. At its centre were churches and a market. Private and commercial buildings developed along streets. From its beginnings, Charlottetown was a nexus of activity, a market town that was the core of an agricultural community. Islanders would travel to Charlottetown to sell produce at the marketplace and to purchase their needs.

The first market was constructed where Province House now stands. In 1823, the Round Market was built, where butter, eggs, meat, potatoes, oats, hay, and fish could be purchased on Wednesdays and Saturdays. In 1867, the Mark Butcher Market House opened at the centre of town, burning to the ground in 1902. In 1904, a market, designed by William Critchlow Harris, opened. The second floor housed a theatre, destroyed by fire in 1958. Today, the farmers' market is near the University of Prince Edward Island on Belvedere Avenue.

Charlottetown was also a place of entertainment, ranging from theatrical performances, to public punishment, such as whippings and hangings, which were performed on the hanging hill that stood on Euston Street between Prince Street and Malpeque Road in Charlottetown. The centre of administration and government, Province House, was constructed between 1843 and 1847 at the centre of town. It was called the Colonial Building until 1873, when the Island joined Confederation. It is still the Island's government and legislative building, and a national historic site.

The early residents of Charlottetown were mainly from Great Britain. In 1784, American Loyalists settled there as well, fleeing the United States during the America Revolution, choosing to remain loyal to Great Britain. By the 1820s, many Irish also lived in the capital city of Charlottetown. In 1841, the majority of immigrants had been born in Ireland, others were English and Scottish. Some of the Loyalists had brought their Black slaves with them. A number of escaped slaves and free Blacks came as well. There was never really a separate Black community on the Island, but many Blacks lived in The Bog, an economically deprived, racially mixed section of Charlottetown. The Lebanese population also left a distinctive mark on the city of Charlottetown: many became peddlers and then began commercial enterprises—mainly corner stores, many of which still exist today.

The most difficult problem was deciding which location would make the best capital... I finally chose Charlottetown. It is near the middle of the Island and its three rivers provide easy travel to the interior. A small stream runs through Charlottetown and provides pure drinking water. The site is also easily defended. The cannons at Fort Amherst control the harbour.

Captain S.J. Holland 1765

Originally cast in 1875, the bell known affectionately as "Big Donald" was moved from the city market building to the tower of city hall in 1888. Named in honour of fire chief Donald MacKinnon who served from 1875 to 1879, it was brought from the tower to its present location next to city hall in 1966.

*Facing page:
A performance by the Confederation Players in front of Province House, where the Fathers of Confederation first met in 1864. Confederation itself, however, was initially met with resistance by Islanders and the Island government.*

Between 1800 and 1870, ships were built on the Charlottetown waterfront, leading to the construction of warehouses, sail lofts, and the residences of shipowners and shipbuilders. Charlottetown was the residence of many people involved in shipbuilding, even if their businesses were centred elsewhere on the Island. A great fire destroyed much of the commercial district in 1866. Rebuilding took place, changing the look of the town. The commercial district shifted and became centered on the block between Queen and Great George Streets. In 1884, another fire took its toll and architects such as William Critchlow Harris and Phillips and Chappell were employed in the rebuilding, developing buildings along Victoria Row.

Because Province House in Charlottetown was the location of the Charlottetown Conference in September 1864 that led to Confederation, the city is sometimes called "the birthplace of Confederation." Although Charlottetown hosted the initial discussions of the terms of agreement of Confederation, the province did not join

the Dominion until 1873, when the debt associated with the railroad forced the Island to accept the terms. The subsequent completion of the railway changed the lifestyle and look of the town, further establishing it as a centre of communication, economy, and transportation.

Charlottetown has gone through great change during the past 200 years, growing in population and diversity. It is still a cultural centre, home to independent theatre, art galleries, and a vibrant literary scene. The Confederation Centre of the Arts opened in 1964, on the site of the historic farmers' market. Each summer the Charlottetown Festival features the musical *Anne of Green Gables*, based on the novel by Lucy Maud Montgomery. The Confederation Centre Art Gallery and Museum, the largest art gallery east of Montreal, is the location of an extensive collection of visual art and sculpture, historic and contemporary, the collection of Robert Harris portraits, sketches, and notebooks, and manuscripts such as the original hand-written texts of Lucy Maud Montgomery.

A boardwalk now skirts the waterfront of Charlottetown at Victoria Park, as the rising sun bathes the harbour with fresh light.

Facing page: The Confederation Centre of the Arts was built in 1964 at the centre of Charlottetown in the site of the historic market. Interpreting and celebrating Canada's cultural heritage through the arts, it is the home of the Confederation Centre Art Gallery & Museum, as well as the annual Charlottetown Festival, featuring the musical Anne of Green Gables.

*Today, restored
nineteenth-century
heritage properties on
historic Great George
Street house businesses
and the Inns on Great
George. The street,
running from the
waterfront to Province
House, is also the
location of St. Dunstan's
Basilica, and its
sidewalks were once
walked by the Fathers
of Confederation.*

Over the last three centuries, vessels spanning canoes, sailing ships, ferries, freighters, and sailboats, have passed the red sandstone coastline of Charlottetown Harbour.

Destination Prince Edward Island

An aerial view of Charlottetown.

Ship to Shore

Looking at Prince Edward Island, it is obvious why shipbuilding flourished. The exceptional number of bays and protective coves for harbours were important during the mid-nineteenth century and Prince Edward Island's age of sail. Between 1840 and 1890, over 3,100 wooden vessels were constructed in 176 locations. This area of Prince Edward Island, roughly from Bedeque on the southeast to Portage in the west bordered by Egmont, Bedeque, and Malpeque Bays was the focus of much shipbuilding. The growth of Summerside, its main centre, is directly tied to the shipbuilding industry.

The town of Summerside developed at the edge of Bedeque Bay, serving the agricultural, shipbuilding, and fishing region that surrounded it. By 1861, Summerside was the chief port of trade to New Brunswick. The town was a major shipping port, and main commercial and service centre, serving the wider agricultural area of the western portion of the Island, which had a lesser population density due to its slow settlement and its isolation. When shipbuilding declined, the town was the centre of a booming silver fox farming industry. Mansions still stand attesting to these times of affluence. Later, it was home to a now closed Canadian Forces Base.

Summerside was incorporated as a city in 1995. Today the city's history and culture is captured in various ways. Eptek National Exhibition Centre is located on Summerside's waterfront. Opened in 1978, the gallery features historical and art exhibits, as well as the Island's Sports Hall of Fame. Summerside is also home to the Wyatt Centre and to the International Fox Hall of Fame and Museum, exploring the fox-raising industry of the

I am the furrows turned red in the autumn,
I am the seagull's delight.
I am the cow path that leads to the stable,
I am the owl in the night.
I am the spruce tree,
and I am the crow....

"Your Island Will Disappear"
Allan Rankin

last century. The College of Piping is an important institution and site of the Summerside Highland Gathering during the last week of June. Throughout the community, artists are capturing the history of the are in murals on the side of Summerside buildings.

This region includes the narrowest point of the Island—six kilometres wide—separating Malpeque and Bedeque Bays, which was used by the Mi'kmaq as a portage passage. It is thought the major concentration of Mi'kmaq on the Island was on or near the Bedeque-Malpeque isthmus. This area was settled by Acadians during the French period, who dyked and farmed the area's marshlands. In the 1780s, the area was settled by United Empire Loyalists, but today, it is still part of the Evangéline region, the Island's Acadian centre, where the Acadian tradition, culture, and language flourish.

Evangéline was the main character of Henry Longfellow's 1847 poem, which describes the deportation of the Acadians. In the poem, Evangéline Bellefontaine is separated from her lover, Gabriel Lajeunesse, during the deportation from Grand Pré, and the two spend the rest of their lives searching for one another. The tale is a definitive one for the Acadian community in the Maritime region, including Prince Edward Island.

The Evangéline area has its own distinct history and character. The main source of livelihood here is the inshore fishery, mainly in Egmont and Bedeque Bays. Its unique identity and flavour is created by Acadian communities with festivals and institutions such as restaurants, theatres, and museums. West of Summerside is Miscouche, the location of the Acadian

The Acadian flag is a powerful symbol of the Acadian community, made up of the descendants of the early French settlers who established Acadie in the 1600s.

Facing page:
Le Promenade Giftshops in the Acadian community of Wellington, as well as sites such as the Handcraft Co-op in Abrams Village, and the popular dinner theatre, Cuisine à Mémé, at Mont Carmel, represent the rich Acadian history and culture in the Région Évangéline.

museum offering genealogical information about Island
Acadians, their history and way of life from 1720 to the
present. Also found there are artifacts of Acadian tradition—paintings, photographs, farm tools, textiles,
quilts, journals, and manuscripts. Other cultural landmarks are the Acadian village at Mont Carmel, Abram's
Village Handcraft Co-op, and the popular dinner theatre featuring Acadian performers—Cuisine à Mémé.

Wellington is also an Acadian community. The town
was once known as Quagmire, when John Barlow purchased a farm and established grist and saw mills in
1859. It was renamed in honour of the Duke of Wellington, and the town grew up around Barlow's mills. The
carding and grist mills were dismantled after 1937. The
sawmill was the last of the Barlow enterprise to remain
in operation until 1965. Near the pond at the centre of
town where the mills stood is a park and monument
commemorating the site of the mills. Along the shore
of Malpeque Bay is a commemoration of another aspect
of the area's industrial past—shipbuilding. Here is the
Green Park Provincial Museum as well as Yeo House,

originally built around 1865, the restored house of
James Yeo and family who were involved in the shipbuilding trade.

The landscape and residents of the area of Tyne
Valley have been preserved in music—particularly in
that of Larry Gorman, a reknowned traditional Island
songwriter. He was notorious for writing biting satiri-
cal songs about the people and lives he saw around him,
providing historical information about Island life. His
work as a songmaker has been studied by folk music
researchers, such as Sandy Ives, from the University of
Maine. Each summer, the Larry Gorman Festival is held
in Tyne Valley.

On the north shore, Lennox Island is the location of
the Mi'kmaq Nation reserve, where 250 members of the
Lennox Island band live. Mi'kmaq language and stories
have been kept alive through elders, though few members speak the language. The Lennox Island band oper-
ates a commercial peat moss operation, an oyster co-op,
and a craft outlet. A small museum features
murals of Mi'kmaq legends.

Summerside, a community that developed around shipbuilding, today is growing as a cultural centre in the western portion of the Island. It is the location of the Eptek National Exhibition Centre featuring historical and art exhibits, the Jubilee Theatre, as well as the Island's Sports Hall of Fame. Nearby is the College of Piping and Celtic Performing Arts and the Lefurgey Cultural Centre, used for diverse arts activities.

Facing page: Traditional music practices such as fiddling are very much alive and thriving in Island kitchens, ceilidhs, and festivals, as shown by this performance of young fiddlers at the annual Acadien Festival at Abrams Village.

Memory is made public in this large mural on the Summerside Fire Hall, depicting the blaze that swept through the community in 1906.

Pioneer cemetery at Église Notre Dame in Mont-Carmel.

Sunsets and Seascapes

This is the region called by Islanders "Up west" or West Prince. It begins at Portage and takes in the mainly fishing and farming community, up to North Cape. Most residents are descendents of the Acadians, Scots, and Irish who were the first European settlers. The area is geographically and historically diverse. The land has facilitated use for potato farming as it is flat or has gentle hills. Much of the interior is covered with woodland and the eastern coastline along Cascumpeque Bay has deep indentations, created by rivers. On the western side, the coast has spans of white sand as well as red sandstone cliffs that are sculpted by the powerful forces of wind and water. Because of its relative distance from the centre, this area is less developed and in some ways, more pristine and culturally distinct.

There's horses in the water and horses on the road
And here comes old Russell Aylward and he's
haulin' up another big load
And the party lines are ringin', and the word
keeps passin' on
You can hear them roar from the Tignish shore
There's moss in Skinner's Pond.

"Song of the Irish Moss"
Tom Connors

The natural harbour offered by Cascumpeque Bay was the site of a Mi'kmaq settlement and later became the site of a French fishery. French explorer Jacques Cartier may have first come ashore in 1534 in this area of the Island. Jacques Cartier Provincial Park commemorates this potential contact. Up the coast is the town of Alberton, a major site of the silver fox industry. On an offshore island, now called Oulton's Island, Robert Oulton and Charles Dalton first succeeded in domesticating silver foxes. They called their business Cherry Island Ranch. The boom eventually collapsed due to over-production, and changes in fashion. A monument to the industry and fox houses still stand in West Prince.

Towards the northern point is the community of Tignish, built by Acadian and Irish settlers. People in the community depend mainly on fishing for their livelihood. Because the town lies inland, fishers use the Judes Point wharf, the largest fishing port on the Island. Like many of the institutions in Tignish, the fishery is a successful co-operative. This early co-op was started in 1924 by local fishermen who wanted to break the domination of the private lobster canning companies. The first fishermen's union was formed in Tignish. The community is still a major lobster and fish processor and centre for commercial tuna fishing. The wharf itself is built around a saltmarsh, with the fishery buildings on several docks. The strength of the co-operative tradition is apparent in the range of co-op institutions found here—like the supermarket, the sawmill, feed mill, gas station, health centre, and credit union. The Church of St. Simon and St. Jude is a sign of the strong Roman Catholic religious tradition of the area.

Jutting out into the sea, dividing the water of the Gulf of St. Lawrence and the Northumberland Strait, is North Cape. Irish moss is still gathered from the shores here in traditional fashion: horses are used to rake the moss from the surf. The moss is then dried and shipped away for the extraction of carrageenan, a thickening product. The lighthouse at North Cape was once the only building there. Now a restaurant, an interpretive centre, and a gift shop stand at the cape. The area is also a test site for windmills run by the National Research Council.

On the west coast are several fishing communities. Miminegash is the site of the largest fishing wharf on the Island's west coast. Irish moss is harvested along this coast as well, and an interpretive centre is located in

Oyster fishers on Foxley Bay.

Facing page: Alberton Museum is located in a former town courthouse; erected in 1878. Now a national historic site, it contains displays of artifacts of early residents, photos illustrating the history of Alberton and its inhabitants, and extensive genealogical information on area families.

Miminegash. Howard's Cove is the location of a striking formation called Giant's Armchair, a rock resembling a chair, fashioned out of stone by wind and water. At Cape Wolfe, Elephant Rock once stood. Sculpted by the elements into a convincing elephant form, it drew many visitors. These same forces recently removed the elephant's trunk, a sign of the ever-changing natural and tourist landscape.

At West Point is the Cedar Dunes Provincial Park. The West Point lighthouse completed in 1876 watches over a shore surrounded by tales of local shipwrecks, buried treasure, mysterious sea guns, and sea serpents. Members of the community now run a restaurant and hotel in the lighthouse. While the uses of many landmarks like these have changed, some remain the same. In Bloomfield, a woollen mill is still in operation. MacAusland Woollen mill stands near the waterfall on the Mill River from which it drew its power. Today, the mill depends on electricity to card, spin, and weave wool into warm blankets.

West Point light with its unusual black and white stripes stands at the western entrance to the Northumberland Strait. The traditional red and white stripes of the tallest lighthouse on the Island were changed in 1915, so they would show up more clearly against the vivid sunsets at West Point.

Facing page: Restored Historic Sea Rescue Station at Northport, used in the rescue of the crew of the A.J. MacKean in a gale in 1906. A memorial to the Northport and Alberton rescue teams stands nearby.

Detail of a door, at the side entrance of the Saint Simon and Saint Jude Catholic Church, Tignish. The large church was built in the mid-1800s by its first pastor, Peter McIntyre, entirely from Island brick.

Destination Prince Edward Island

Sunrise at Fox Island, near the Elite Seed Farm, a source of the Island's potato seed.

Traditional crafts remain a fixture of the present as illustrated by these hooked rugs at the Prince County Exhibition, Alberton.

Destination Prince Edward Island